TALES FROM THE BEDSIDE

PUBLISHED BY
JOHN WISE, RN, BSN
PO BOX 5104
CLEARWATER, FL
34618-5104

ISBN 0-9643043-0-9

987654321

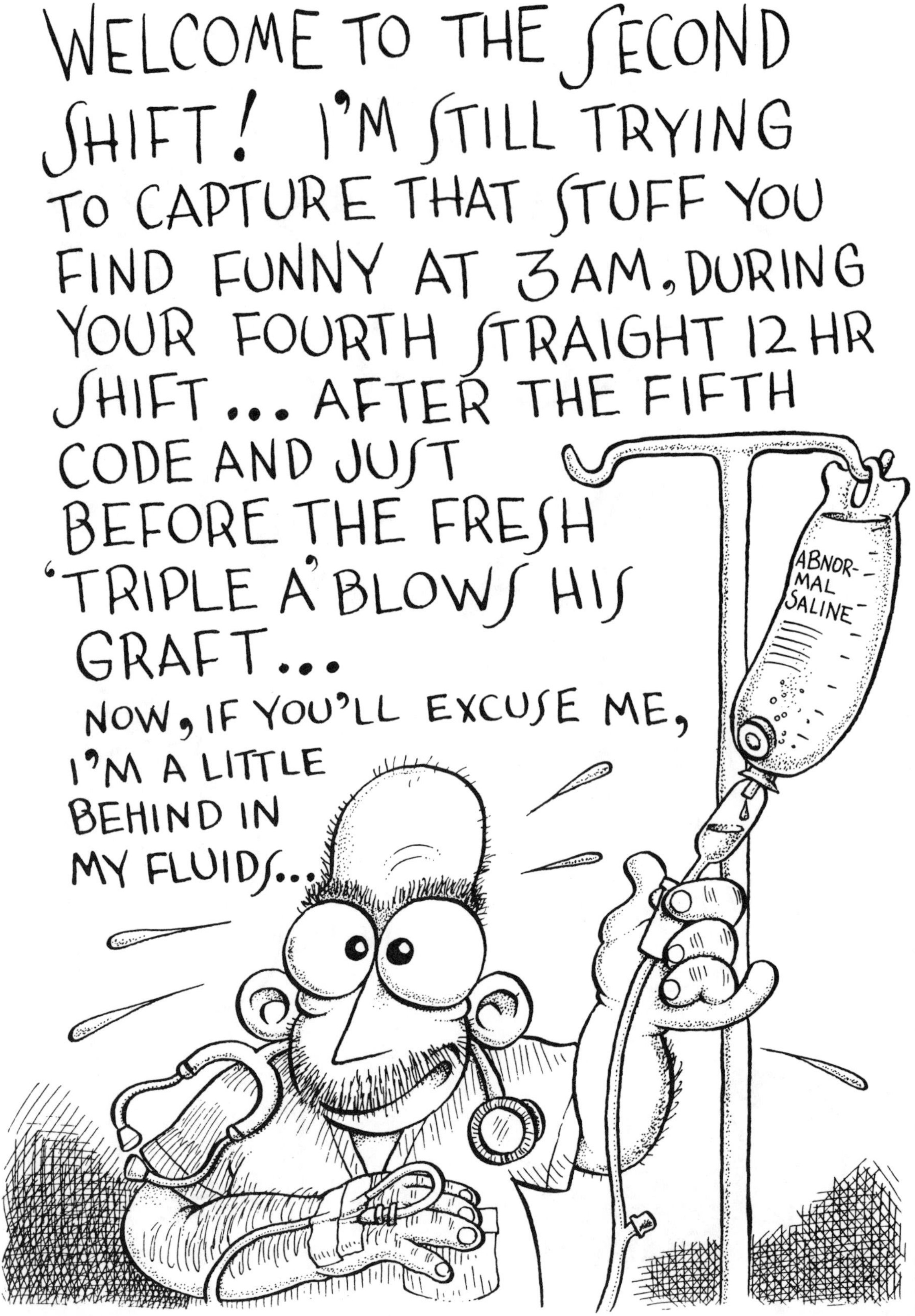
WELCOME TO THE SECOND SHIFT! I'M STILL TRYING TO CAPTURE THAT STUFF YOU FIND FUNNY AT 3AM, DURING YOUR FOURTH STRAIGHT 12 HR SHIFT... AFTER THE FIFTH CODE AND JUST BEFORE THE FRESH 'TRIPLE A' BLOWS HIS GRAFT...
NOW, IF YOU'LL EXCUSE ME, I'M A LITTLE BEHIND IN MY FLUIDS...
ABNORMAL SALINE

ALIEN ABDOCTION

*EUTHANASIA

GENERAL SURGERY 101

9

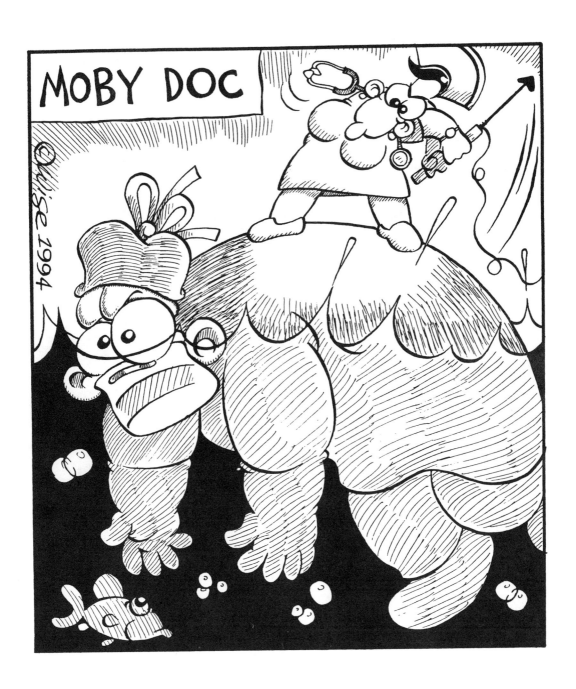

"I SAID I WON'T BE IN TODAY, I'M COMING DOWN WITH SOMETHING!"

SPERM BANK ROBBER

PINOCCHIO'S FORESKIN

©Wise 1994

TEST TUBE TEENAGER

21

22

OLD MACDONALD HAD A PHARMACY
MOO MOO HERE
OINK OINK HERE
E-I-E-I-
MAC
©Wise 1994

24

27

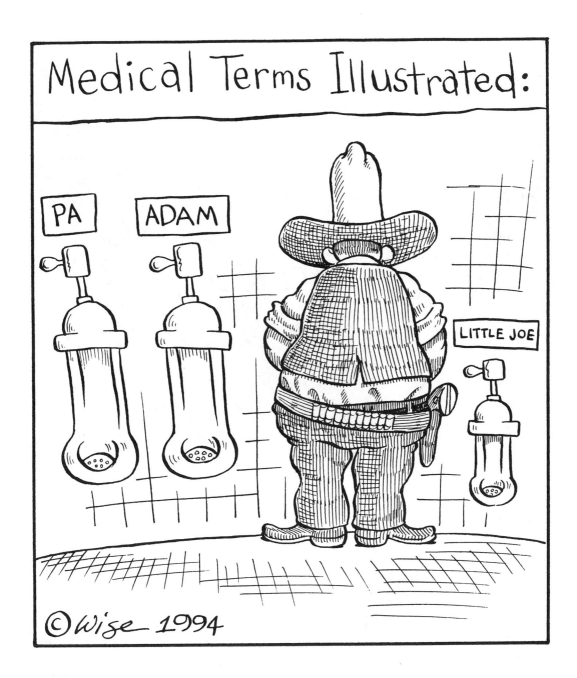

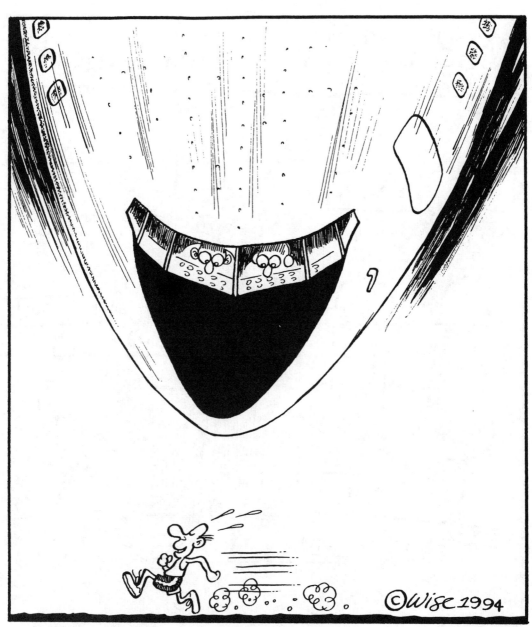

"AT LEAST I STILL HAVE MY HEALTH."

40

©Wise 1994

Peter Pancreas

©wise 1994

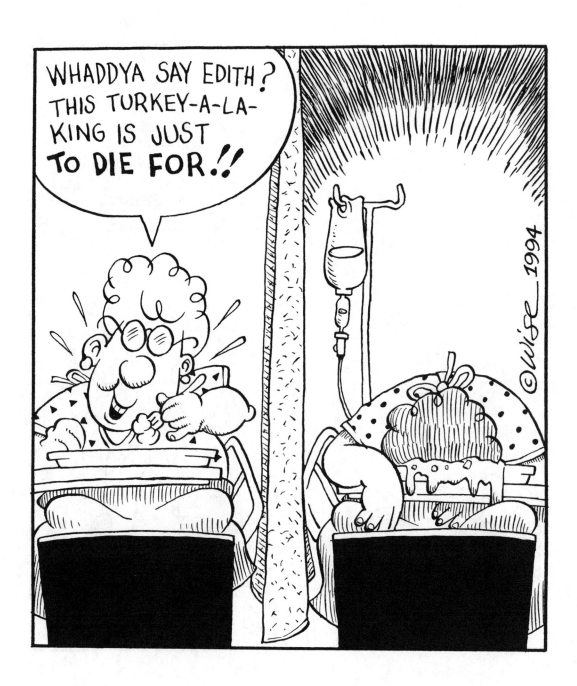

HARE CLUB FOR MEN...

"I HATE MONDAYS!"

SAFE SEX: FOREPLAY

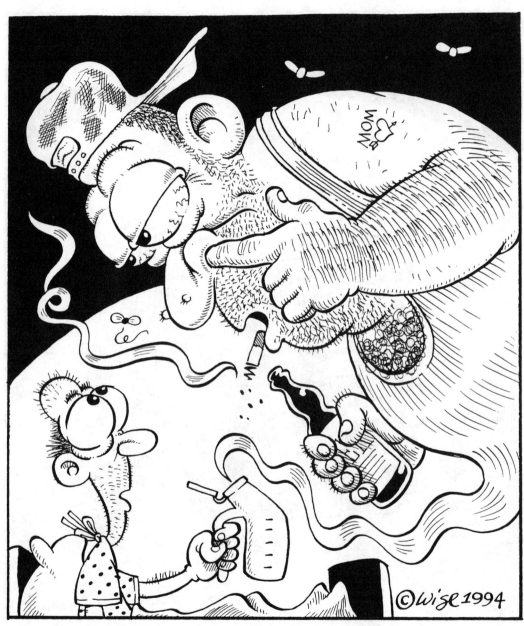

"WHAT KIND OF GENIE DID YOU EXPECT RUBBING YOUR URINAL?"

57

58

59

DOCTOR ASSISTED INSECTICIDE

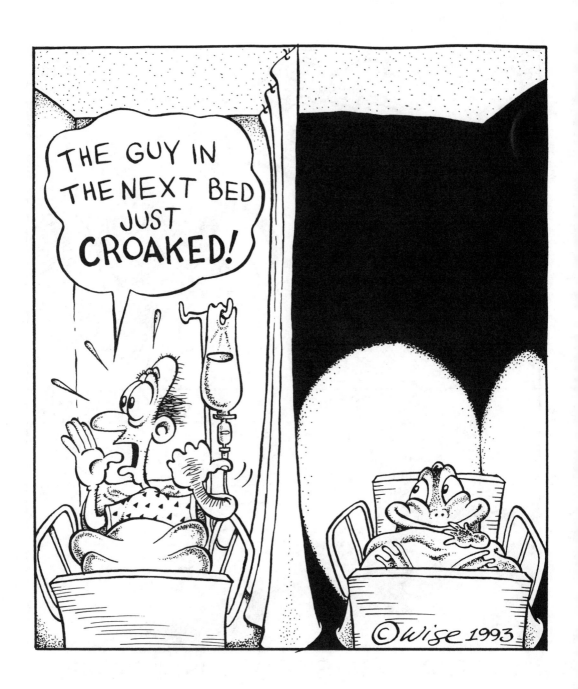

YOU CAN TELL HIS WIFE HE'S COMING
THROUGH WITH FLYING COLORS!!!

IF YOU'RE SO SMART, HOW COME
YOU'RE A DOCTOR?

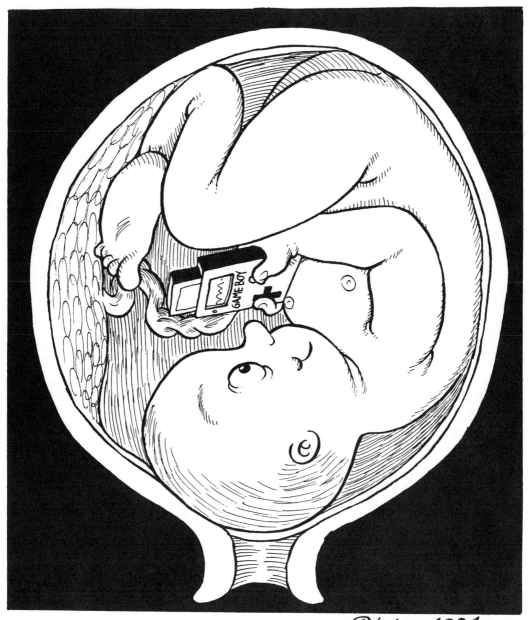

©Wise 1994

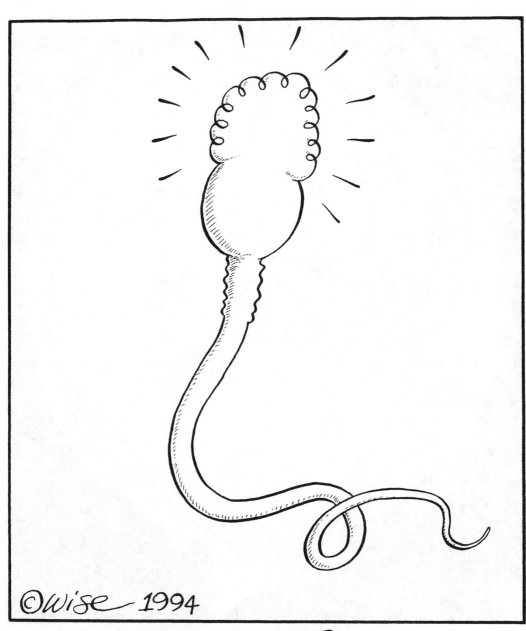

©wise 1994

SPERM PERM

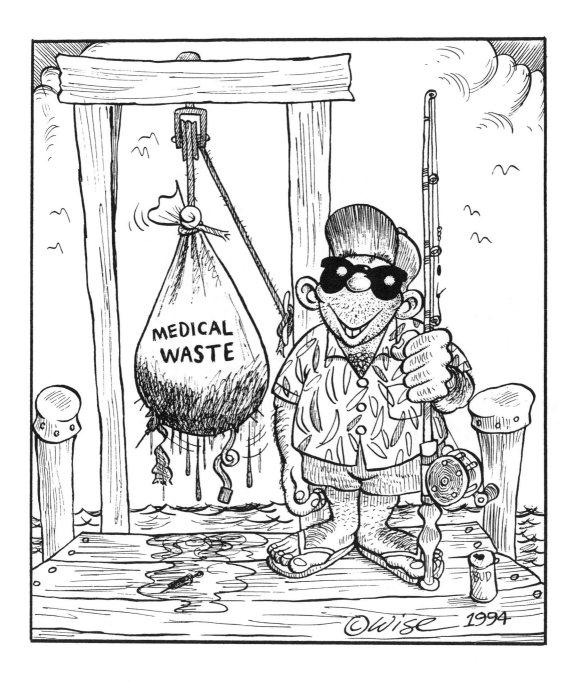

WAS FEELING UNDER THE WEATHER BUT
GOT OVER IT...

74

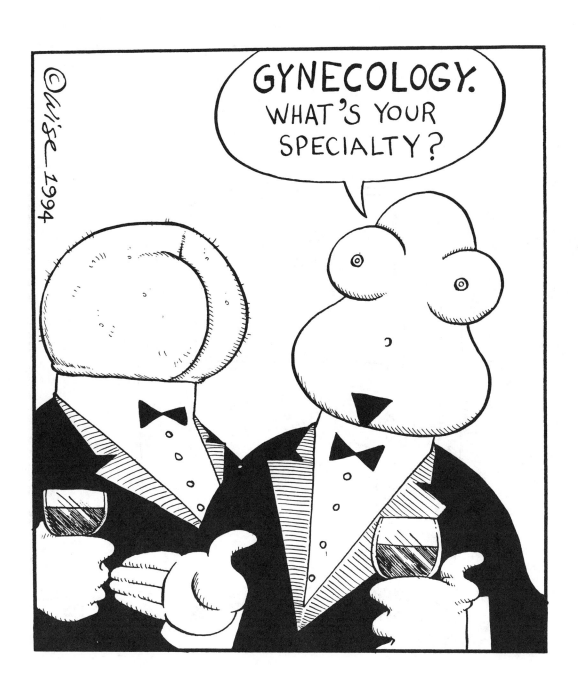

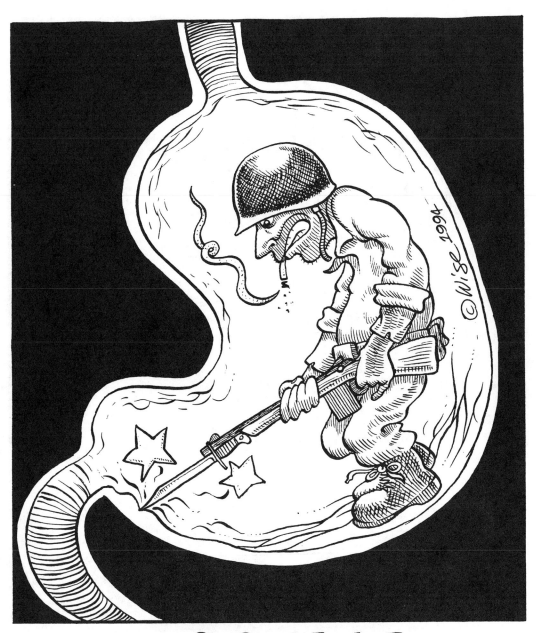

UPPER G.I. JOE

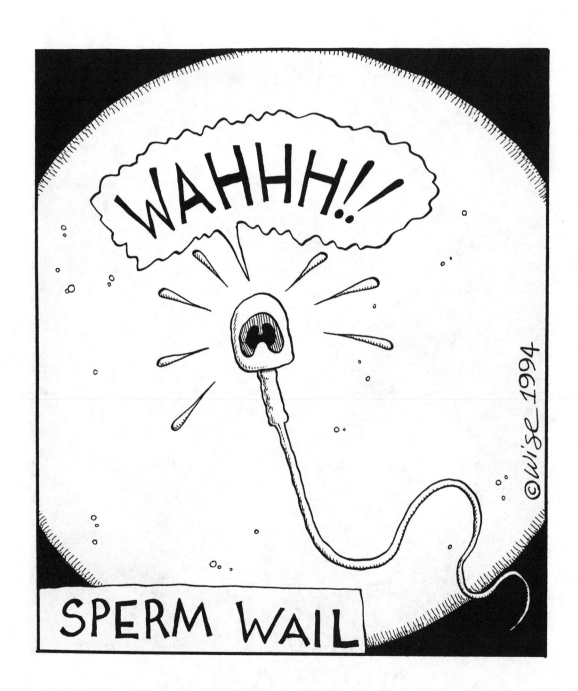

BAD AIR DAY

THE SPERMINATOR

87

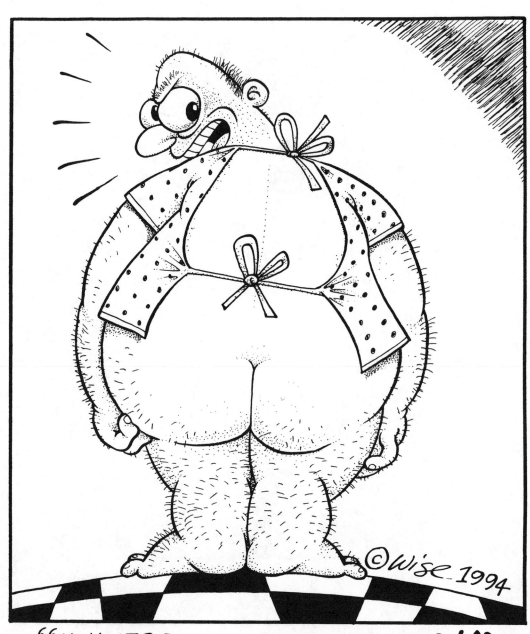

"UNIVERSAL COVERAGE MY ASS!"